AUSSIE SLANG DICTIONARY

Published by Brolga Publishing Pty Ltd
ABN 46 063 962 443

PO Box 452
Torquay Victoria 3228
Australia
admin@brolgapublishing.com.au

National Library of Australia Cataloguing-in-Publication entry

      Aussie slang dictionary : easy guide to Aussie slang /
      compiled by Lolla Stewart.
      9781925367669 (pbk.)
      English language – Australia – Slang – Dictionaries.
      427.994

Cover design by David Khan
Typeset by Imogen Stubbs
New quotes for updated editions collated by Christine Fotis

BE PUBLISHED

Publish through a successful publisher.
National Distribution, International Distribution to the United Kingdom, North America
Sales Representation to South East Asia
Email: markzocchi@brolgapublishing.com.au

Compiled by Lolla Stewart

A

A bit more choke and you would have started: said to somebody who has just passed wind loudly.

A over T: short for arse over tit, meaning upside down or head over heels.

Ace: excellent.

Acid: the good word: the truth. *The good acid.*

Ac/dc: bisexual.

Act the goat: to behave foolishly.

Adam's ale: water.

Add insult to injury: to make matters even worse than they already are.

Aerial ping-pong: Australian Rules Football. A reference to the

spectacular leaps which players can make to 'mark' the ball.

After dark: rhyming slang for shark. *Watch out for the after dark.*

Aggro: aggressive. *He got aggro with me.* Also used as a noun: *she was really givin' me the aggro.*

Airy fairy: vague.

Akubra: broad-brimmed Aussie hat made out of pressed rabbit fur and worn by farmers and famous golfers!

Alf: stupid person.

Alice, The: Alice Springs, Northern Territory town near Uluru (Ayers Rock).

Alley up: to pay back a debt.

All froth and no beer: superficial, without substance.

Alligator: a horse.

Alligator pear: avocado. Named for

the reptile like skin of the fruit and the pear like shape.

All over him/her like a rash: refers to a person who can't keep their hands to themselves.

All over red rover: completely finished.

All over the place like a mad woman's breakfast: a mess; in a state of chaos.

All wool and a yard wide: authentic; trustworthy.

All your Christmases have come at once: a bonus of good luck.

Alone like a country dunny: alone; lonely; abandoned.

Amber fluid: beer.

Ambo: ambulance or ambulance driver.

Anchors: brakes of a vehicle.

Angle of the dangle: the state of an erection.

Ankle-biter: a toddler; small child.

Ants pants: looking good, similar to *the bees knees*.

Anyhow mate: a saying used to change the subject of a conversation, or signal leaving due to boredom.

Any tick of the clock: very soon, any time now.

ANZAC: acronym for Australian and New Zealand Army Corp. Refers to WWWI soldiers (called diggers) who were the first ANZACs, and generally to Australian soldiers.

Apeshit: to express extreme anger. *The boss went apeshit when I arrived late.*

Apples (she'll be): everything will work out okay.

Apple eaters: refers to someone who lives or is from Tasmania (apple growing state).

Apple Isle: Tasmania.

Argie-bargie: testy; argumentative.

Argue the toss: to question a decision. *There's no point arguing the toss with me, son.*

Around the twist: insane.

Arse about face: back to front.

Arse around: to fool around; to muck about; to waste time.

Arse off: to depart; to leave.

Arse over tit: trip or fall over.

Arvo: afternoon.

Aussie: shortened form of Australia/ Australian.

Aussie battler: an ordinary Australian trying to make ends meet.

Aussie salute: brushing flies away from the face with your hand.

Australian as meat pie: authentic.

Autumn leaf: a jockey who continually falls off.

Avago: have-a-go. To attempt or try to do something.

Away with the pixies/birds: day dreaming; in another world.

Awning over the toy shop: male beer belly, with the toy shop referring to the genitals.

Axle grease: money.

Ay: hey, hello or used to signal when you haven't understood what someone is saying.

EEEEK!

B

Baccy: tobacco.

Back blocks (out in the): beyond suburbia and the more established farm and cattle properties.

Backchat: to answer impertinently a person in authority, or parent.

Back door bandit: uncomplimentary term for a homosexual male.

Backhander: a bribe; underhand payment.

Back o' Bourke: outback; remote country area.

Back of beyond: outback Australia.

Bad case of the trots: diarrhoea.

Bag: an ugly woman or to criticise

something, similar to *knock*.

Bagman: swagman; tramp; drifter.

Bagman's gazette: mythical source of bush rumours.

Bag of fruit: rhyming slang for suit.

Bail out: to leave.

Bail up: to hold up, rob, earbash or confront someone.

Bald as a bandicoot: having no hair.

Ball and chain: the wife as referred to in her absence.

Balls: testicles.

Balls-up: used when something goes terribly wrong. *The club awards night was a complete balls-up.* The reference is to testicles, not toys!

Bananas: to be crazy with anger. *Shazza went bananas the other night when I told her about the car.*

Banana-bender: Queenslander.

Bangs like a dunny door in a gale: refers to a woman free with sexual favours. Also see "D" for dunny.

Bang on: to hit the target right in the middle, right/correct.

Banged up: pregnant.

Banjo: frying pan; shoulder of mutton.

Barbie: barbeque.

Barcoo buster: outback Queensland term for a wind from the west.

Bar flies: (old) men who hang around the pub all day.

Bark at the lawn: to vomit. *Let me through, fellas! I gotta go bark at the lawn.*

Barmy as a bandicoot: insane.

Barney (to have a): fight, scuffle or argument.

Barrack for: to support a sports team, or player. *I barrack for the Kangaroos.*

Bastard: can be used in both a positive and negative way. *He was a real bastard!* Or *Long time no see, you old bastard!*

Bash: noun for a wild party; verb to punch, to attack someone or something. *He bashed the livin' daylights out of it.* Also *she gave me a real ear bashing.* Meaning she nagged or scolded.

Basket case: hopeless, emotionally broken. After he lost his job he became a real basket case.

Bastard from the bush: a country boy, a yokel.

Bat: an ugly woman.

Bathers: swimming costume.

Bats: crazy; insane.

Battery acid: cheap white cask wine, tastes like vinegar.

Battler: usually referred to as *the little Aussie battler*: an individual struggling against the odds to make a better life, but never getting ahead.

Bazza: nickname for Barry. Also a general term for the Aussie bloke. Names such as Garry, Darren, Sharon, are shortened in a similar way to Gazza, Dazza, Shazza.

Bazzaland: Australia.

Beanie: close fitting woollen knitted hat.

Beak: magistrate, judge or your nose.

Bearded clam: a description of the female genitals.

Beat around the bush: to go around the topic, avoid the point in question.

Beaten by a blow: shearer slang referring to the running of shears from one end of a sheep to the other.

Beaut, beauty : great, excellent.

Beer gut: bulging or fat stomach.

Beer o'clock: the end of the work day when you go to the pub for a beer.

Bee's dick: smallest possible margin. *He won by a bee's dick. Or you've got a bee's dick chance of winning, mate.*

Bee's knees: the best.

Beg yours?: pardon me?.

Belly-buster, belly/whacker: stomach-first dive in water. Ouch!

Belly-up: refers to the failure of a venture or enterprise or death.

Belt: to hit or punch.

Belt up: stop talking, be quiet.

Belyando spew: shearer's illness, usually associated with poor cooking conditions.

Bend the elbow: to drink a bit too much. He bends the elbow a bit doesn't he?

Bender: a drinking spree.

Bent as a scrub tick: crazy; foolish.

Berko: furious, mad. *She went berko at me.*

Better half: the spouse. *Dave, meet my better half.*

Better than a poke in the eye with a burnt stick: not as bad as the alternative; an admission that things could be worse.

Bewdy: similar to beaut. Means very good or excellent. *You got the beer? Bewdy!*

Bible-basher: over enthusiastic evangelical Christian.

Big bickies: a large amount of money.

Big note oneself: to boast or brag.

Big smoke: the city.

Big sticks: the goal posts in Aussie Rules football.

Bike (the town): a reference to a promiscuous woman.

Bikkie/bickie: biscuit.

Billabong: a waterhole.

Billiard ball (as sharp as a): not perceptive, mentally slow.

Billy: tin container with handle for boiling water over a campfire.

Billy Bluegum: a koala.

Billy cart: a go-kart, often homemade for children to use.

Billy lids: rhyming slang for kids.

Billyo: fast, with great speed. *He took off like billyo with the dog chasing him.*

Bin: prison; gaol.

Bindy: grass burr or nettle.

Binge: like a bender, a drinking spree.

Bingle: a minor car accident.

Biscuit: cookie.

Bite on (to put the): ask/pressure someone for money.

Bite your bum: shut up; get lost.

Bities: collective term for insects that bite, ie. spiders, bull ants.

Bit more choke and your would have started (a): refers to a person who has just farted loudly.

Bitser: a dog of mixed parentage, a mongrel. Refers to *bits of this, bits of that.*

Bizzo: business. *Mind your own bizzo.*

Black stump: a mythical place that signifies the edge of the outback. *The road goes way beyond the Black Stump.*

Bleeder: man (derogatory term).

Bleeding oath: expression of unqualified agreement.

Blimey: an expression of surprise. *Blimey! Did you see that 'roo?*

Blind Freddie: mythical person representing the lowest common denominator in comprehension skills. *The punchline was so obvious, Blind Freddie could have seen it coming.*

Bloke: a man. Generally a positive label.

Bloodhouse: a rough pub.

Blood'n'blister: sister (rhyming slang).

Blood's worth bottling: refers to a person of uniquely admirable qualities.

Bloody: the great Australian adjective in widespread use. Serves to emphasise the word that follows it. *Bloody good! Bloody awful! Bloody hell! It's about bloody time!*

Bloody oath: an agreement. *Will we strike? Bloody oath we will!*

Blotto: blind drunk.

Blow a fuse: to lose one's temper.

Blow in the bag: to take a breathalyser test.

Blower: the telephone.

Blowie: blow fly, the large, droning kind.

Blow-in: an uninvited guest.

Blow through: leave in a hurry.

Bludge: to sponge off someone or the system.

Bludger: a person who doesn't make an effort but takes something for nothing.

Blue: a fight or an argument or a red-headed person.

Blue (make a): make a mistake.

Blue duck: disappointment; mistake.

Blue-flier: a fast kangaroo.

Blue Heeler: the police or a breed of dog.

Blue-nosed wowser: killjoy; party-pooper; teatotaller (non-drinker); someone who kills the mood or ruins a party.

Blues: the police.

Bluestone college: Pentridge Prison.

Blue-tongue: shearer's term for a shed hand – an unskilled worker.

Bluey: a swag, a rolled up blanket OR an infringement notice issue by the police.

Bobby dazzler: someone or something excellent.

Bob's worth/two bob's worth: opinion; point of view.

Bob's your uncle: a summary way of expressing that things are, or will be, fine. *We'll bring the booze, your bring the food, we'll meet at the beach and Bob's your uncle.*

Bodgy: of inferior quality.

Bog: the toilet. Also to defacate.

Bogan: cultural sub-group who listen to old rock music, generally own pit bull terriers and have late-eighties haircuts. A rough type of individual.

Bogged: stuck car, usually in mud or sand.

Bog house: toilet.

Bog in: to commence eating.

Bog roll: toilet paper.

Bog standard: basic; unadorned; without accessories.

Boiler: an older woman. Refers to hens too old to roast.

Boil the billy: to put the kettle on; to make a hot drink.

Bolted: to leave quickly, run off.

Bomb: a car that hardly goes, is rusted out, or is covered in dints and scratches.

Bondi cigar: a turd floating in the sea.

Bondi tram: usually *to shoot through like a Bondi tram:* to leave in a hurry, often leaving unpaid debts.

Bonkers: insane, crazy.

Bonza: top quality, excellent.

Booby: a foolish person.

Boogie board: half size surfboard.

Bookie: bookmaker.

Boomer: kangaroo; or anything excessively large.

Boomerang: a dishonoured cheque – it bounces back.

Boots'n'all: wholeheartedly; all in.

Booze artist: heavy drinker.

Booze bus: mobile police breathalysing station.

Boozer: the local pub or an individual who drinks at the same.

Booze-up: a party with more alcohol than food.

Bo-peep (to go for a): to take a sly look at something that isn't your business.

Bore the pants off (someone): to be excessively boring.

Bot: to scab, to bludge off, borrow with no intention of giving back. *Can I bot a cigarette of ya, mate?*

Botfly: a scrounger; a scab; someone who is always taking but never giving.

Bottle shop/Bottle-O: liquor store, usually attached to a pub.

Bottler: an individual or experience of remarkable quality. Refers to the desire to capture and keep it in a bottle.

Bottom-of-the-harbour scheme: a tax dodge.

Bounce: bully.

Bowerbird: a compulsive hoarder.

Bow wow: really ugly.

Boys in blue: police.

Bradman: sporting opponent who is unbeatable. A reference to the unequalled cricketer, Sir Donald Bradman.

Brain bucket: bicycle safety helmet.

Brazz monkey weather: very cold.

Brass razoo: a negative term meaning having no money. *Don't look at me, mate, I haven't got a brass razoo.*

Breadbasket: stomach.

Break open a coldie/tinnie: to open a beer.

Breakfast bird: a kookaburra.

Breather: a rest. *Let's take a breather, fellas.*

Breeze: an easy task.

Brekkie: breakfast.

Brickie: bricklayer.

Brick short of a load: simple-minded; stupid.

Bride's nightie (up and down like a): referring to something that fluctuates.

Bright as a two watt globe: not very bright person; stupid; dumb.

Bright-eyed and bushy-tailed: describes a person who is in good health and spirits and is rearing to get started on something.

Bright spark: clever; intelligent.

Brizzie/Brisvegas: Brisbane.

Broad in the beam: having large hips and/or bottom.

Broken packet of biscuits (he's a): something or someone who looks good on the outside, but is a mess on the inside.

Brown eye: to show ones bottom, mooning.

Brown-eyed mullet: a poo floating in the sea.

Brown nose: to ingratiate oneself, to fawn, or *crawl*.

Bruce: a general name for a man.

Brumby: wild horse in the bush.

Brummy: counterfeit; dud.

Bubbler: a drinking fountain.

Buckley's: a slim chance, or none at all. *You've got Buckley's, love.*

Budgie smugglers: men's swimming costume. Also known by the brand Speedo.

Buffer: an elderly man.

Buffin' the muffin: sexual intercourse.

Bugger: widespread expression of disappointment. *Oh, bugger!* OR a term similar to bastard and used in both positive and negative ways. *Come here, you old bugger, and give us a hug.*

Bugger-all: nothing or very little.

Bugger off: to shoot through, leave.

Buggered: exhausted, worn out.

Buggered if I know: to have no idea or

know nothing about something.

Buggerlugs: irreverent, but also affectionate name for someone. *Buggerlugs here wants to go home.*

Buggery: mythical place, a long way away, reserved for those whom we tell to bugger off. *He can go to buggery for all I care.*

Bugle: a nose. *That dead fish was a bit on the bugle.*

Built like a brick shit house: someone or something strong.

Bullamakanka: mythical place in the outback.

Bull bar: metal bar fixed to the front of a vehicle (typically a 4WD) to protect it from hitting kangaroos. Also known as a *roo bar*.

Bull dust: a lie.

Bull's wool: misleading information.

Bully for you: derisive exclamation.

Bum: backside, bottom.

Bum fluff: adolescent's first growth of facial hair.

Bum nuts: eggs.

Bummer: a let-down or disappointment.

Bundy: Bundaberg rum.

Bun in the oven: pregnant.

Bunch of fives: a fist. The same thing as a knuckle sandwich.

Bung: broken, not working or to place something carelessly. *Just bung it over there.*

Bung it on/bung on an act: to act with attitude.

Bunyip: a mythical Aboriginal bush spirit animal that lives in swamps and billabongs.

Burl: to attempt something. *I'll give it a burl.*

Burl along: to hurtle along; to keep going regardless.

Burr up: get angry.

Bush: the countryside; any rural area.

Bush baptist: a heavily religious person.

Bush bash: to go off road in a vehicle, forcing your way through untouched bush.

Bush carpenter: self-taught carpenter or tradesman whose work is slap-happy or crude.

Bush dinner: damper and black tea.

Bushed: exhausted; lost; tired.

Bushfire blonde: a redheaded person.

Bushie (also bushwhacker): farmer or country dweller of straightforward nature.

Bushman's clock: a kookaburra.

Bushman's hot dinner: damper and mustard.

Bush oyster: nasal mucus.

Bush pig: an unattractive person.

Bushranger: outlaw; thief of the bush; outback criminal.

Bush telegraph: gossip; grapevine.

Bush telly: campfire.

Bushweek: a fictional time when everybody slacks off and everything goes wrong. *Hurry up, you lot. What do you think this is, bushweek?*

Bushytailed: full of health and good spirits; awake bright and early in the morning.

Busy as a centipede on a hotplate: very busy.

Busy as a one legged bloke in an arse kicking contest: to be doing nothing.

Butcher's/butcher's hook: from rhyming slang meaning a look. *Take a butcher's hook at that poor bastard.*

Butcher's canary: fly (insect).

Butterfly: a coin that fails to spin when tossed.

B.Y.O.: bring your own alcohol to a restaurant.

C

Cabbage patcher: resident of Victoria.

Cack-handed: left handed.

Cackleberry: an egg.

Cactus: ruined; no good for anything. *We can't use my car, it's cactus.*

Cakehole: mouth.

Call it a day: the end; to finish what you're doing and go home.

Call 'Ralph': to vomit.

Camp as a row of tents: a homosexual male.

Cancer stick: cigarette.

Cane toad: a Queenslander.

Can't take a trick: describes a person who has a run of bad luck.

Captain Cook: rhyming slang for a look.

Cark it: to die.

Carn!: come on! An encouraging cry to your sports team. *Carn the Bombers!*

Carpet grub: a small child, often at the crawling stage.

Carpet muncher: a lesbian.

Carry on like a pork chop: to behave in a silly manner, or to express frustration or anger out of proportion to the problem.

Carry the mail: to buy drinks, normally at a pub or bar.

Cat's hiss: rhyming slang for piss.

Cat's pyjamas: refers to a person who thinks they're better than others. *He thinks he's the cat's pyjamas.*

Caustic crackers and strawberry sand: to have marriage and/or relationship problems.

Chalkie: teacher.

Charge like a wounded bull: to ask ridiculously high prices.

Charge like the light brigade: same as above, very expensive fee structure.

Chateau de cardboard: cask of wine.

Cheap as chips: inexpensive.

Cheap drunk: someone who becomes drunk quickly, normally only after one or two drinks.

Cheapskate: unwilling to spend money.

Cheerio: goodbye.

Cheese and kisses: rhyming slang for the missus; the wife.

Chew and spew: a cheap cafe.

Chew the fat: to have a good chat.

Chewie: chewing gum.

Chewie on your boot!: an Australian Rules Football cat-call inciting the player to miss when going for a goal.

Chiak: to tease, pour scorn on or generally muck about.

China plate: rhyming slang for mate.

Chinwag: gossip, natter.

Chippie: a carpenter.

Chockers, chock-a-block: as full as is possible. *I couldn't eat another thing. I'm chockers.*

Chokkie: chocolate.

Choof off: to leave.

Chook: a hen; a chicken.

Chook house: chicken pen.

Choom: an Englishman.

Chop (not much): expresses disappointment in something. *The weather's not much chop today, eh?*

Choppers: teeth; dentures.

Chrome dome: a bald man.

Chromo: a prostitute.

Chuck a sickie: calling in sick to work when you're not sick.

Chuck a U-ie: execute a u-turn.

Chuck up: to vomit.

Chuck a wobbly or spaz: to throw a temper tantrum.

Chunder: vomit.

Chunderous: nauseating.

Clackers: teeth.

Clagged out: worn out; dead

Clagged the bag: worn out; dead.

Clanger: a 'faux pas'; a conversation stopper. *She dropped a clanger when she asked how much it cost.*

Clayton's: a substitute; not the real thing.

Cleanskin: an unlabelled bottle of wine, generally of not-bad quality. Also refers to cattle that have not been branded.

Click: kilometre. *It's 10 clicks away.*

Climb the wall: to go mad.

Clinah/cliner: girlfriend; woman.

Clobber: clothing; to hit hard. *She clobbered him one.*

Clodhoppers: feet.

Clucky: experiencing maternal urges.

Clued up: well informed.

Cluey: smart, knowledgeable.

Clumsy as a duck in a ploughed paddock: very clumsy; crude; inelegant.

Coathanger, the: Sydney Harbour Bridge.

Cobber: mate.

Cobbler: last sheep to be shorn.

Cock and bull: something that is a lie. *He told me it was free, what a cock and bull.*

Cockatoo: a person posted to keep lookout during illegal activities.

Cockatoo weather: fine by day, rain at night.

Cocky: farmer.

Cocky's joy: golden syrup (similar to maple syrup).

Cockroach: a person from New South Wales.

Codger: an old man.

Codswallop: rubbish; a lot of nonsense.

Coffin nail: a cigarette.

Cold and dark as a bushman's grave: very cold and gloomy.

Cold as a mother-in-law's kiss: very cold or unwelcoming.

Coldie: chilled beer.

Colonial oath!: an emphatic agreement.

Come a cropper: fall flat on one's face.

Come a gutser: to make a mistake; to have an accident.

Come in spinner!: call during a betting game of two-up.

Comic guts: rhyming slang for stomach or guts.

Compo: workers' compensation.

Conchie: someone who is conscientious.

Cooee: bush call, especially when lost; also means the distance covered by the call. *There isn't a tree within cooee of here.*

Cook: a wife.

Cook the books: fiddle with the accounts in a business; falsify the figures

Coolgardie safe: early form of refrigeration, where foodstuffs were kept cool inside a wooden frame covered with wet hessian. Named after a Western Australian mining town.

Coot: short for bandicoot, usually refers to someone unlikeable.

Cop: to be on the receiving end of something. *He copped a belting from his dad.*

Coppertail: an ordinary person.

Cop shop: police station.

Cop it sweet: to take punishment like a

man; to enjoy good fortune.

Corker: excellent; big. *The fish I caught was a corker.*

Cornstalk: a person from New South Wales.

Corroboree: Aboriginal ritual dance.

Cot case: very ill; highly intoxicated; bed ridden.

Cotton on: to understand; to pick up the meaning of something.

Cough drop: idiot.

Could eat a horse and chase the rider: very hungry.

Could kick the arse off an emu: in very good health.

Couldn't fight his way out of a paper bag: refers to a weak or inept person.

Couldn't get a kick in a stampede: said of a poorly performing football player.

Couldn't give a continental: denotes lack of concern.

Couldn't give away cheese at a rats' picnic: utterly hopeless.

Couldn't hit the side of a barn: someone with poor aim.

Couldn't knock the skin off a rice pudding: physically weak; ineffectual.

Couldn't lie straight in bed: refers to a crooked or devious person.

Couldn't organise a screw in a brothel: refers to an inept individual.

Couldn't run a chook raffle in a country pub: thoroughly incompetent; someone with no organisational skills.

Couldn't win if he started the night before: a slow racehorse/individual.

Could sell boomerangs to the Aboriginals: Australian take on *could sell ice to the Eskimos* – very persuasive.

Counter lunch/Countery: lunch from a pub.

Country cousin: rhyming slang for a dozen.

Couple of pies short of a grand-final: not all there; mentally deficient.

Cow cockie: dairy farmer.

Cow juice: milk from a cow.

Cows come home (waiting 'til the): waiting all day.

Cozzie: swimming costume.

Crack a fat: to get an erection.

Crack onto (someone): to hit on someone; to pursue romantically.

Cranky: in a bad mood.

Crap: excrement; shit.

Crapper: the toilet.

Crash hot: first rate; excellent; very good.

Crawler: a sycophant; a person trying to gain favours.

Creeping Jesus: an evangelical Christian.

Cripes/crikey: exclamation.

Croak/croak it: to die.

Crock: lies.

Crockery: teeth.

Crocodile: a horse.

Crook: a felon; ill. *The cops caught the*

crook. I feel real crook today.

Crooked as a dog's hind leg: devious individual; a line that isn't straight as it should be.

Crow-eater: someone who lives in South Australia.

Crown jewels: male genitalia.

Cruddy: something of low quality.

Crumb gatherer: an AFL player who is good at getting the loose ball.

Crumblies: frail old people.

Crust: job or income. *What do you do for a crust?*

Cubby house: small, timber house in the garden for children to play in.

Cultural cringe: national inferiority complex regarding Aussie artistic accomplishments when compared to the rest of the world.

Cuppa: cup of tea or coffee.

Curly: nickname for a bald person.

Curry (give someone a bit of): give someone a hard time.

Cush: fair and square.

Cushy: a soft and well rewarded job.

Cut lunch: sandwiches.

Cut lunch commando: army reservist.

Cut snake (mad as a): someone so upset they could do anything.

D

Dad'n'Dave: rhyming slang for shave.

Dag: a person of an eccentric or amusing nature; a scruffy individual.

Daggy: unfashionable.

Daisy cutter: term for a ball that is thrown or kicked very low.

Daks: trousers or underpants.

Damage: cost; amount owed. *What's the damage for the meal?*

Damper: bushman's bread made from flour, water and salt.

Dander: rhyming slang for anger.

Dark on: to be angry about something.

Darling shower: dust storm.

Darwin pyjamas: no pyjamas.

Darwin stubby: a very large bottle of beer.

Date: arse, bottom, behind. *Get off your fat date.*

Dead as mutton chops: dead.

Dead but won't lie down: a persistent person.

Dead dingo's donger (as dry as a): very dry.

Dead horse: rhyming slang for sauce; a defunct cause or argument. *I think you're trying to flog a dead horse, mate. Give up!*

Dead marine: empty beer bottle.

Deadset: without a doubt.

Dead sinker: a long glass of beer.

Dead to the world: in a deep sleep, commonly alcohol induced.

Deener: shilling (a pre-decimal coin).

Dekko: a look.

Derro: a down and out person; a homeless person.

Dick head: idiot.

Dicky: of doubtful qualities; risky.

Diddle: to swindle.

Didn't bat an eyelid: showed no emotion; gave no reaction.

Didn't come down in the last shower: shrewd; quick witted.

Digger: gold miner or ANZAC (serviceman).

Digs (your): your house.

Dill: idiot.

Dilly: dotty; idiotic.

Dilly-bag: a food bag or a small bag to carry things.

Dingaling/dingbat: foolish individual.

Dingdong: a foolish person; noisy argument.

Dingo's breakfast: a yawn, a leak and a good look around.

Dingy: a small aluminium boat.

Dink/double dink: to take a second person on a bicycle. *C'mon, I'll dink ya.*

Dinkum: genuine; authentic.

Dinkum oil: inside information; true.

Dinky di: authentic; real.

Dip out: to fail or withdraw.

Dipstick: an idiot.

Dish licker: dog.

Dishy: glamorous.

Divvy up: to divide; to separate into lots.

Divvy van: police wagon.

Do a flit: to run away or escape responsibility.

Do a Melba: to continually return from retirement.

Do a perish: to die.

Do me a favour: a remark that indicates you want another person to stop making comments.

Do the dirty: to do the wrong thing by someone.

Do your block: to lose your temper.

Do your dash: to reach one's limit.

Do your lolly/na-na/nut: to lose your temper.

Dob: to inform upon someone; to tittle-tattle.

Dobber: one who informs upon others, generally held in contempt.

Doco: documentary.

Docket: bill; receipt.

Doesn't give a bugger: couldn't care less.

Doesn't know if he's/she's Arthur or Martha: someone who is stupid or in a state of confusion.

Doesn't miss a trick: a very alert person.

Dog and bone: telephone.

Dog box: an old fashioned train with no corridors.

Dog's breakfast: chaos; a mess.
It was all over the place like a dog's breakfast.

Dog's eye: rhyming slang for meat pie.

Dole bludger: somebody on social/ government assistance when unjustified.

Done deal: something that is done or finished.

Done like a dinner: thoroughly defeated.

Dong: to strike someone.

Donger: penis.

Donk: motor car engine.

Donkey's years: a very long time.

Don't come the raw prawn: don't try to con or fool me.

Don't do anything I wouldn't do: joking advice to someone going somewhere.

Don't pick your nose or your head will cave in: contemptuous advice to a person exhibiting a complete lack of brains.

Dooks: fists.

Doona: duvet, eiderdown or comforter.

Dosh: money.

Doss-house: boarding house.

Down the hatch!: a popular drinking toast.

Down Under: Australia.

Dial: face.

Drag the chain: to slip behind in a drinking contest.

Draw the crabs: to attract unwelcome attention.

Dribs and drabs: bit by bit. *The school kids arrived in dribs and drabs.*

Drip: stupid individual. *Don't be a drip.*

Drippy: boring.

Drink with the flies: to drink alone.

Drive the porcelain bus: to vomit into the toilet bowl.

Drives uphill with the clutch slipping: someone stupid.

Drongo: a real idiot. Refers to a racehorse of the same name who was famous for running last.

Droob: slow witted person, similar to nong, drongo and drip.

Drop a clanger: to make a social blunder or say something inappropriate.

Drop-bears: mythical creatures which fall from trees onto tents at night – a tale to scare young campers.

Drop-kick: a slow-witted individual. *He's a real drop kick, that one.*

Drop off!: go away.

Drop your bundle: to lose control, to have a nervous breakdown.

Drop your guts: to fart/pass wind.

Drover's dog: disparaging reference to the lowest common denominator in capabilities. *It was so easy a drover's dog could have done it.*

Drown some worms: to go fishing.

Drum: information; tip-off. *I'll give you the drum.*

Dry as a dead dingo's donger: very dry or thirsty.

Dry as dog biscuits: something that is very dry and unpleasant to eat.

Dubbo: a country bumpkin.

Duchess: sideboard.

Ducks and drakes: rhyming slang for snakes.

Ducks and geese: rhyming slang for police.

Duck's dinner: a drink of water without anything to eat.

Duck's disease: having a long body but short legs.

Duck shoving: pushing into a queue; dodgy business practice.

Dudder: con-man.

Dud-dropper: someone who sells cheap stuff as good stuff because it is stolen.

Duds: trousers.

Duffer: silly. An affectionate term.

Dull as a month of Sundays: extremely boring.

Dummy (to spit the): to get very upset.

Dumper: a wave that breaks suddenly on top of surfers and swimmers.

Dunga: angry.

Dunking: dipping a biscuit into a cup of tea or coffee.

Dunlop cheque: a cheque that bounced. Refers to a famous rubber company.

Dunny: a toilet, especially an outdoor one.

Dunny brush: a 'flat top' haircut.

Dunny budgie: fly (insect).

Dunny diver: a plumber.

Dunny rat (cunning as a): a very sly individual.

Durry: cigarette; tobacco.

Dusting: trashing; beating.

Dust-up: a brawl or fight.

E

Ear-basher: someone who talks and talks; a bore.

Earwig: to eavesdrop.

Easy as pushing shit uphill with a toothpick: extremely difficult if not impossible.

Easy as spearing an eel with a spoon: extremely difficult.

Eat the crutch out of a low-flying duck (could): a description of hunger.

Eau de cologne: rhyming slang for telephone.

Egg beater: helicopter.

Egg boiler: bowler hat.

El cheapo: something that is cheap and nasty; a cost cutting individual.

Elephant's trunk: rhyming slang for drunk.

Emma chisit: how much is it? What does it cost?

Emu parade: a rubbish collecting activity organised in school grounds.

Enzed: New Zealand.

Esky: a portable ice cooler.

Even stevens: equal chance or amount.

Every bastard and his dog: absolutely everybody.

Evo: evening.

Expeno: expensive.

Eyes on, hands off: alright to look, not ok to touch.

F

Face fungus: facial hair, ie. a beard or moustache.

Face like a chook's arse: a miserable expression.

Fag: cigarette.

Fair cow: a really annoying person or event.

Fair crack of the whip!: give me a fair go.

Fair dinkum: an exclamation of disbelief or surprise.

Fair go mate: statement you make when someone is not letting you do or say something.

Fair suck of the sauce: a call for even handedness. *Fair suck of the sauce, mate, let the kid have a go.*

Fairy: male homosexual.

Fairy bower: rhyming slang for shower.

Fang carpenter: dentist.

Far gone: beyond repair; madly in love; drunk.

Farmer Giles: rhyming slang for piles; haemorroids.

Fat chance: when someone has little or no chance of happening.

Feed the chooks: to submit to a barrage of reporters and TV cameras and give out information.

Feral: a hippie or something disgusting.

Few stubbies short of a six pack: lacking in intelligence.

Fibber: a teller of lies.

Figjam: acronym for *F*** I'm Good, Just Ask Me*. A person who has a high opinion of themselves.

Fit as a mallee bull: in good health, strong.

Five finger discount: shoplifting.

Fizzer: something that peters out or doesn't meet expectations.

Flat out like a lizard drinking: working extremely hard; very busy.

Flake: shark meat for sale in a fish and chip shop.

Flake out: to collape from exhaustion or intoxication.

Flaming thing/flaming good time: extra bad or extra good.

Flash as a rat with a gold tooth: over dressed.

Flat chat: really busy.

Flat out like a lizard drinking: doing something very fast.

Flat to the boards: extremely busy; working non-stop.

Flemington confetti: rubbish.

Flick: to give something, or someone the flick means to get rid of them in an abrupt manner.

Flicks: the movies.

Flip your lid: to get angry.

Floater: meat pie in a bowl of green pea soup and/or gravy (South Australian delicacy!); a turd.

Flog: to sell something or to steal the

same item! Can also mean to beat another sports team hands down.

Flog the cat: to indulge in self pity.

Flog the log: to masturbate.

Flophouse: accommodation for homeless people.

Flounder spearer: musical conductor (orchestra).

Flu bog: jam.

Fluff: to make a minor error; to fart.

Flutter: a small bet.

Flying the Aussie flag: to be out in public with your shirt tails untucked and hanging loose.

Flynn (in like): to go into something (especially seducing women) with great enthusiasm and haste. Refers to early Australian movie actor, Errol Flynn.

Fly wire: gauze flyscreen covering a

window or doorway.

Folding stuff: paper money.

Footy: Australian Rules Football.

For crying out loud: an expression of annoyance.

For fun and fancy to please old Nancy: an expression used to answer the question 'What are you doing?' when you don't want to tell the truth.

Fossick: to look for surface gold.

Fossick around: search a little aimlessly for something.

Four'b two: rhyming slang for Jew.

Four'n twenty: a popular brand of meat pie; an underage girl offering sexual favours. Also refers to four minutes of fun and twenty years of goal.

Fox: a term given to a drinking partner who leaves before they have to buy a round of drinks.

Franger: a condom.

Fred Nerk: your average citizen, John Doe. Similar to Joe Blow.

Free (a): penalty kick awarded in Australian Rules Football.

Freebie: to get something for nothing.

Fremantle doctor: cool breeze that blows into Perth and Fremantle each afternoon.

French letter/Frenchy: a condom.

Fridee: Friday.

Fried eggs: small breasts.

Frocks: older ladies dresses.

Front: audacity, cheekiness.

Fruit loop/cake: a stupid person.

Fuck truck: a panel van, usually fitted out with speakers and a mattress and proudly owned by a lusty young male. Similar to *Shaggin' Wagon*.

Full as a boot: very drunk.

Full as a goog: overindulged in food; gorged.

Full as a seaside dunny on Boxing day: to have consumed too much alcohol. Refers to the public conveniences on a crowded beach on December 26.

Full as a state school: bloated.

Full of beans: energetic.

Full up to pussy's bow: to have eaten one's fill; bloated.

Fun bags: a woman's breasts.

Funny as a fart in a phone box/ elevator: not amusing.

Funny farm: mental institution.

Furphy: a red herring; a false report.

Further back than Walla Walla: way beyond schedule; last by a long way.

G

'G (the): a shortened form of M.C.G which is the shortened form of the Melbourne Cricket Ground.

Gabba (the): nickname for the Brisbane Cricket ground which is in the suburb of Wooloongabba.

Galah: a person behaving like an idiot. The original galah is a pink and grey Australian parrot.

Galah occasion: an event that requires

formal dress.

Galoot: usually called a big galoot. Another variation on the individual behaving badly. Similar to droob, drip and drongo.

Game as a piss ant: extremely brave.

Game as Ned Kelly: bold as brass and a bit of foolhardy. Ned Kelly was a daring bushranger in Victoria's early days.

Gander: a look. *Take a gander at that, will ya.*

Garbo: garbage collector.

Gargle: a drink.

Gasbag: someone who can talk a lot.

Gazunder: a chamber pot (it 'goes under' the bed).

G'day: famous Australian greeting, equivalent to *Hello* or *Hi*.

Gee and tee: a gin and tonic (drink).

Geebung: a native born Australian living in a remote area.

Geek: a look.

Get off your bike: to lose control of your temper.

Get on like a house on fire: to strike up a friendship; to enjoy each other's company.

Get on your goat: to irritate or annoy.

Get the arse: to be fired from a job.

Get the axe: to lose your job.

Get the drift: to comprehend.

Get the Guernsey: to receive an award or recognition.

Get your arse into gear: someone is asking you to get a move along or hurry up; get organised.

Get your dander up: to become enraged.

Gibber: enormous plains in the outback covered with small pebbles, mostly red in color.

Ginger Meggs: rhyming slang for legs; also the name for someone with red hair.

Gink: a silly person.

Give it a burl: have a go at something.

Give someone Bondi: to beat them up.

Give something the flick: to dispose of it; get rid of it.

Glutton for punishment: someone who goes back for more hard or unpleasant work.

Gobsmacked: surprised; amazed.

Go bush: to take yourself out of circulation, go to ground for a while, not necessarily in the country.

Go crook: to vent your anger.

Go down the gurgler: to fail in a business venture or enterprise.

Godzone: meaning God's own, Australia. This term is also claimed by New Zealanders.

Gob: mouth.

God botherer: religious fanatic. Similar to *Bible basher*.

Go for the doctor: to take action.

Going off: something that is a lot of fun. *The party was going off.*

Going like hot cakes: something selling fast.

Going to see a man about a dog: said when one does not want to reveal where they are really going.

Going to see a star about a twinkle: going to the toilet.

Go like the clappers: to work or take off very fast.

Go mulga: to go bush.

Gone on someone: in love with that person.

Gone to the dogs: something or somplace that is no longer any good.

Gone troppo: to go mad or to have lost all sense of civilisation after spending too much time in the tropics.

Good as gold: excellent.

Good nick: to be in a good state of repair, or good health.

Good-oh: okay; good; agreement of satisfaction.

Good on ya!: good for you!

Good sort: an attractive person.

Go through like a dose of salts: to work very fast.

Got space to sell between the ears: brainless.

Go two rounds with a revolving door (couldn't): a weak or ineffectual person.

Go walkabout: to go missing.

Gong: denotes something past its usefulness. *The old motor's had the gong.* Refers to a signal of failure in a talent quest.

Grave jumper: someone who takes someone else's job or seat.

Grazier: sheep or cattle farmer.

Great Australian salute: swipe at flies around one's face.

Green around the gills: easily given to nausea and vomiting.

Greenie: environmentalist.

Gregory Peck: your neck.

Grey ghost: parking inspector.

Grey nurse: rhyming slang for purse.

Grin and chronic: rhyming slang for gin and tonic.

Grizzle/grizzle guts: complaining person.

Grog: alcohol.

Grog on: to drink.

Grommet: junior surfer.

Grot: dirty or untidy.

Ground parrot: a small farmer.

Grouse: fantastic; excellent.

Grub: someone or something dirty.

Grumble bum: an old whinger.

Gub/gubbah: an old Aboriginal term for a white person.

Guffing off: someone who is lazy.

Gully: a small valley.

Gullyraker: a cattle thief.

Gumboot: rubber boots, Wellingtons or a condom.

Gummy: toothless.

Gumpuncher: a dentist.

Gumsucker: someone who lives in Victoria.

Gundabluey: a heavy downpour of rain.

Gunner/gunna: an individual who procrastinates, who is always *gunna* (going to) do something but rarely does.

Gunyah: a humpy (badly built cottage or shed, often made out of found objects).

Gurgler: plughole.

Guzzle: to drink something quickly.

Guzzler: an alcoholic.

Gyp: (pronounced jip) to swindle.

H

Haggle: try to talk the price down.

Hair like a bush pig's arse: wild, unkept hair.

Hair of the dog: drinking more alcohol as a cure for a hangover.

Hairs on ya chest (to put): something you eat or drink that will (supposably) make you more of a man, or something scary.

Handles like a dog on lino: handles badly.

Hang out: spend time together.

Halfback flanker: rhyming slang for wanker. Refers to a playing position in Australian Rules Football.

Half pinter: a small person.

Ham and eggs: rhyming slang for legs.

Handbrake: a term used by a husband when his wife slows him down, usually on shopping trips.

Happy as a bastard on Father's day: depressed; miserable.

Happy as a box full of birds: in high spirits.

Happy as a boxing kangaroo in a fog: very miserable.

Happy as a pig in mud: very happy.

Happy as Larry: very pleased; content.

Hardcase: someone who is close minded.

Has a death adder in his/her pocket: a tight fisted person; a miser.

Has a few palings missing from the fence: simple, not all there or mentally unstable.

Has a Japanese bladder: has to urinate frequently.

Has a snout on (someone): to hold a grudge.

Has white ants in the woodwork: mentally unbalanced.

Hasn't got a bean/cracker: broke.

Hasn't got all four paws on the mouse: slow witted.

Hasn't got an earthly: has no chance or idea.

Hatter: someone who lives alone.

Have a slash: to urinate.

Have a snort: to have an alcoholic drink.

Have a sticky/sticky beak: to pry.

Haven't got two bob to rub together: broke.

Haven't they fed the dingoes lately: a greeting to an unexpected guest.

Head like a mini with the doors open: to have large or protruding ears.

Head like a robber's dog: very ugly person.

Heaps: a lot. *He had heaps of beer.*

Heart starter: first alcoholic drink of the day.

Heave: to vomit.

Heebie-jeebies/screaming heebie-jeebies: terror; an awful fright.

Hen fruit: eggs.

Hey diddle diddle: rhyming slang for middle and piddle.

Hide the sausage (play): sexual intercourse. *Bazza's playing hide the sausage with Shazza.*

High as a dingo's howl: fowl smelling.

Hip pocket nerve: a reference to the area where men keep their wallets and the taxpayer's sensitivity to government imposed charges. *The new tax will really hit the hip pocket nerve.*

Hit the hay/sack: go to bed/sleep.

Hit the frog and toad: to hit the road, usually said by a visitor when they are ready to leave.

Hit your kick: open your wallet.

Home and hosed: finished the task well.

Hooks: fingers.

Hooley: a wild party.

Hoon: a lout or a lair in a (usually loud) car; to drive around with a loud exhaust and a squeal of tires to draw attention to oneself.

Hope your balls turn into bicycle wheels and back pedal up your arse: a colourful curse.

Hooroo: goodbye.

Hooter: nose.

Horizontal exercise/dancing: sexual intercourse.

Horses for courses: fitting the right person to a particular task.

Hotter than a shearer's armpit: unpleasantly hot.

Hottie: hot water bottle.

Hot under the collar: to get angry.

Howzat!: expression used by cricketers when appealing for a batsman to be given out. From *how's that!*

Hubby: husband.

Humdinger: something excellent.

Hump a bluey: old term for carrying a swag.

Humping: having sex.

Humpy: a rough-made shack or lean-to in the bush.

Hung like a Mallee bull: well endowed male genitals.

Hungry as a black dog: very hungry; famished.

I

I hope your chooks turn into emus and kick your dunny door down!: An Australian curse.

Iceberg: a die-hard swimmer who goes in the water all year round.

Icy pole: popsicle.

Idiot box: the television.

Iffy: of doubtful merit or risky, perhaps of suspicious origins. *The weather looks* *a bit iffy. The plan sounds iffy to me.*

If he laughed, his face would fall off, or crack: a dreary/very gloomy person.

If his brains were dynamite they wouldn't blow his hat off: refers to someone with limited intelligence.

If it was raining palaces, I'd be hit on the head by a dunny door: I'm about as unlucky as you can get.

Ikey: a Jew. Refers to an early Tasmanian convict named Ikey Solomon, the Fagan of Dickens fame. Also can mean miserly, ungenerous. *My grandfather's real ikey.*

I'll be buggered: an expression of surprise or amazement.

I'll be a monkey's uncle: an expression of surprise.

Illywhacker: con man.

In a tizz: in a state of confusion or confused excitement.

In good nick: in good shape; fit and healthy.

In like Flynn: successful.

Innings: life span. Refers to a team's time at the wicket (chance to score) in cricket.

In the cactus: in trouble.

In the club/pudding club: pregnant.

In the nick: in jail.

In ya boot!: I don't agree – so there!

Iron lung (wouldn't work in an): a lazy individual.

Iron out: to knock someone unconscious.

Irrits: to be irritated or annoyed immensely. *She really gives me the irrits.*

Is the Pope a Catholic?: it's true, don't doubt it!

It's a freckle past a hair: a response when someone asks for the time and you're not wearing a watch.

I've seen a better head on a glass of beer: an insulting description of someone you consider to be ugly.

Ivories: your teeth or to the play the piano. *He sure can tickle the ivories.*

J

Jackass: kookaburra.

Jack of: tired of. *I got jack of her borrowing my car.*

Jack of all trades: someone who is good at a bit of everything.

Jack of all trades, master of none: a person that will try anything.

Jack and jill (i will fix your): to pay the bill.

Jackaroo: young drover/stockman in training on a country station.

Jack/jimmy dancer: cancer.

Jack up: to refuse to do something.

Jaffle: toasted sandwich with sealed edges.

Jam jars: thick lensed spectacles.

Jarrah jerker: a Western Australian timber worker.

Jeeze: exclamation. Refers to Jesus.

Jerry: pot under the bed that you urinate in at night.

Jesus wept!: an exclamation.

Jiffy: a moment; short space of time.

Jiggered: broken, useless or doesn't work.

Jillaroo: female jackaroo.

Jimmy riddle: rhyming slang for piddle.

Jimmy Woodser: solitary drink or a lone drinker.

Jocks: male underpants.

Joe Blake: rhyming slang for snake.

Joe Bloggs: average guy.

Joe Blow: average bloke.

Joey: baby kangaroo.

Johnny cake: a type of damper.

Journo: journalist.

Jumbuck: merino sheep.

Jumper: sweater or jersey.

Jungle juice: home made booze.

K

Kangaroo hop: the jerky driving of a learner who cannot control the clutch.

Kangaroos loose in the top paddock: an individual who is a bit mad.

Kark it: to die.

Keen as mustard: enthusiastic.

Keep one for ron: keep something in reserve (for later on).

Kelpie: Australian sheepdog.

Kerfuffle: ado, fuss and bother.

Khyber Pass: rhyming slang for arse.

Kick a goal: to have sexual intercourse.

Kick in: to donate to a whip around at the office or social club.

Kiddiewink: child.

Kindy: kindergarten.

King ping: leading figure.

Kip: a brief nap.

Kiss my arse!: exclamation of disbelief.

Kite flyer: a person who passes discredited cheques.

Kiwi: New Zealander.

Knackered: exhausted.

Knee high to a grasshopper: someone short in size/stature.

Knickers: female underwear.

Knock: to criticise or have sexual intercourse.

Knock the dags off a sick canary (couldn't): a person with no strength of effectiveness.

Knockback: a rebuttal or refusal. *He got a knockback from the girl he proposed to.*

Knocked up: pregnant.

Knockers: people who criticise; a woman's breasts.

Knock-off time: the end of the working day.

Knock-shop: a brothel.

Knotted (get): go away.

Know a thing or two: to be well versed in matters, particularly of a sexual nature.

Know if a tram was up him unless the conductor rang the bell (wouldn't): refers to a person who doesn't know what's going on.

Knuckle sandwich: a punch in the mouth.

L

La-de-da: fancy, posh or affecting superior manners.

Lady blamey: a beer glass made from the bottom half of a beer bottle.

Lady's waist: a gracefully shaped beer glass.

Lag: inform, dob.

Lair: a lout who also dresses in a flashy manner.

Lairise around: to behave in a boorish manner to draw attention to yourself.

Lame-brained: someone that is stupid.

Lamington: a small cube of sponge cake, dipped in chocolate and rolled in coconut.

Lamington drive: a fund raising effort.

Larrikin: a likeable lout.

Larry Dooley: mayhem; confusion.

Land shark: a property developer.

Lashing out: going on a spending spree or getting violent/angry.

Laugh at the lawn: to vomit outside.

Lav: abbreviation of lavatory (toilet).

Lead you up the garden path: to lead you astray.

Leak (to take a): urinate.

Leckie: electrician.

Leftie: socialist or communist.

Legal eagle: a lawyer or solicitor.

Leg opener: an alcoholic beverage offered with the intention of reducing a woman's sexual inhibition.

Leg pull: a trick or hoax.

Lemon: something faulty right from the start that leaves a sour taste in your mouth.

Lezzo: lesbian.

Lie doggo: to remain hidden; to avoid work.

Lift doesn't go all the way to the top floor (the): refers to someone who is mentally deficient.

Lights are on but nobody's home: said of a dim wit.

Like a bad smell: an unwanted presence.

Like a possum up a gum tree: totally at home, very happy.

Like a one-legged man at an arse-kicking party: out of place; ill at ease.

Like a shag on a rock: lonely; to stand out in a crowd.

Like a stunned mullet: astounded; immobilised by surprise.

Like a two-bob watch: crazy; erratic. Refers to a cheap time piece in the old currency.

Like billyo: energetically; with great gusto.

Like putting marshmallow into a money box: refers to the difficulty of inserting a less than erect penis into a vagina.

Like the clappers: fast. *That old car still goes like the clappers.*

Like two ferrets fighting in a sack: refers to a woman's large wobbly backside.

Like watching paint dry: refers to a boring event or spectacle.

Lippy: lipstick.

Liquid amber: beer.

Liquid laugh: vomit.

Liquid lunch: midday meal of beer and more beer.

Little beauty/little ripper: a person or thing of excellence.

Little Vegemites: children.

Little boys: saveloys, cocktail sausages.

Little house: an outdoor toilet.

Lit up like a Manly ferry: intoxicated; drunk.

Lively as a blow fly on a winter's day: lethargic.

Living the life of Riley: to live a carefree, luxurious life.

Loaded: very drunk or very wealthy.

Lob in/lob up: to turn up unexpectedly.

Local bike: promiscuous woman.

Local yokel: a well known resident; someone who lives locally.

Lofty: a tall person.

Lolly: a sweet or candy.

Lolly (do your): lose your temper.

Lolly water: watery, sweet drink with or without alcohol.

Long drink of water: someone very tall.

Long neck: large bottle of beer (750mL).

Long paddock: a farmer's term for the grassy land beside the road.

Loo: toilet.

Look like death warmed up: to look very ill.

Looks like an unmade bed: untidily dressed.

Looney bin: mental institution.

Lord or Lady Muck: someone who looks down on others. *Who does she think she is, Lady Muck?*

Lousy: ill or disappointingly poor. *I feel lousy. The dinner was lousy.*

Lousy Bastard: an individual who won't loan money to a friend; a tightwad.

Low as a shark: despicable.

Lower than a snake's belly: the lowest of the low kind of person.

Lucked out: to have bad luck.

Lucky Country: Australia.

Lucky as a bastard on Father's Day: unlucky

Lumbered: to be left with responsibility for something, such as a restaurant bill or rubbish.

Lunatic soup: cheap red wine.

Lurk: a good deal. *She's on a good lurk in that job.*

Lyre bird: a compulsive liar.

M

Mad as a cut snake: insane, crazy and dangerous.

Mad as a gumtree full of galahs: mentally unbalanced; insane.

Mad as a meat axe: crazy.

Maggoty: angry; furious.

Magpie: hoarder.

Mainlanders: this is how Tasmanians refer to their fellow Australian who don't live on their island.

Make a proper galah of yourself: to look an idiot; make a fool of yourself.

Make a quid: to earn a living.

Man in white: the umpire in an Aussie Rules Football game.

Map of (mappa) Tassie: a woman's pubic hair.

Mate: most common form of address, friend.

Mateship: friends sticking together and helping each other out.

Mate's rates: special deals for friends.

Matildas: old term for a swag or rolled up blanket.

Mean as bird shit: tight fisted; not willing to depart with money.

Mexican: a southerner or Victorian (south of the N.S.W. border).

Mick: Roman Catholic.

Mickey (taking the): sending someone up; deflating their ego.

Middle of nowhere: in the outback.

Middy: a 285 ml glass of beer.

Miffed: mildly annoyed.

Milk bar: corner store; small general produce shop.

Mingy: mean; stingy.

Min min: mythical or mysterious lights in the outback.

Missus: wife.

Mediterranean back: back injuries leading to workers' compensation claim. Refers to the alleged prevalence of this condition among migrants.

Mob: group of people; herd of kangaroos.

Mockers: to put the mockers on

someone is to jinx them.

Moke: a horse or donkey.

Moleskin squatter: a working man that has saved enough cash to buy a small sheep farm.

Molly dook/molly dooker: left handed person.

Mondayitis: aversion to going back to work on Monday.

Mongrel: a terrible person; dog of mixed breed.

Monkey suit: formal dinner suit.

Month of Sundays: a long time. *We haven't seen him in a month of Sundays.*

Moosh: your mouth.

Mopoke: a boring person.

More arse than class: more luck than style.

More front than Myers (or David Jones): bold, cheeky, not backward at putting yourself forward!

More movements than a Swiss watch: refers to a shifty devious person.

More than you can poke a stick at: a lot.

Morning glory: the erection a bloke wakes up with in the morning.

Mousetraps in his pockets: a miserly individual.

Mouthful of marbles: plummy or incoherent speech.

Mozzie: mosquito.

Muck about: waste time fooling around.

Mug: a fool; a person easily duped; a person's face.

Mug's game: a situation or activity that brings more trouble than reward.

Mulga (gone up to): gone bush.

Mulga madness: going insane after spending time alone in the outback.

Mundee: Monday.

Munga: food.

Muso: abbreviated form of musician.

Mystery bag: rhyming slang for a snag (a sausage).

My stomach thinks my throat's cut: I'm very hungry.

Myxo: myxomatosis, a rabbit disease created by the CSIRO to destroy Australia's plague of rabbits in the fifties.

N

Nana: banana.

Nappies: diapers.

Nark: an individual who spoils another's enjoyment or pesters and annoys.

Nasho: national service, no longer compulsory.

Nasty piece of work: an unpleasant person.

NCR rating: Number of Cans Required. The number of beers you need to drink before you would consider having sex with someone.

Needie: a horse.

Nelly: cheap wine.

Never-never: the outback of the outback; buying goods on credit.

We'll pay for the Rolls Royce on the never-never.

Nick (in the): naked; in the nude.

Nicked: to have stolen something, or to be arrested. *I nicked a CD and then they called the cops and I got nicked.*

Nick off!: go away, now!

Nick off: to sneak away when you are supposed to stay.

Nineteenth hole: the bar at the golf club.

Ning-nong: Or just plain nong. A dill; a dim wit.

Nipper: young surf lifesaver.

Nippy: chilly.

Noah's ark: rhyming slang for shark.

Noggin: skull.

Non-compos: insensible; unconscious.

From the Latin phrase: *non compos mentis*.

No drama: not a problem.

No hoper: a loser.

Norks: a woman's breasts.

Nose down, bum up: very busy; hard at work.

Nose, on the: smells bad; is dubious.

Nosh up: a large meal.

Not much chop: not very good.

Not a patch on: not as good as something else.

Not an earthly: no chance or no idea.

Not backward in coming forward: a brash person; rude.

Nothing between the ears: stupid.

Not the full quid: mentally deficient;

something missing up top.

Not the sharpest knife in the cutlery drawer: refers to a slow or dull individual.

Not the sharpest tool in the shed: refers to the same unintelligent person as above.

Not what it's cracked up to be: a disappointing standard; not equal to its reputation.

No worries: no problem; she'll be right.

No wukkin' furries: a deliberate spoonerism on no F***ing worries.

Nuddy (in the): totally naked.

Nude nut: a bald person.

Nuggety: small but tough.

Nuggets: testicles.

Nulla-nulla: Aboriginal heavy wooden club.

O

Ocker: uncouth, uncultured loud mouth, the Down Under representative at the Annual Redneck Awards.

Off one's face: drunk.

Off the beaten track: on a road not used very often.

Off like a bride's nightie: to leave very quickly.

Off like a bucket of prawns in the hot sun: something that stinks.

Off like a robber's dog: to depart quickly.

Off-sider: assistant or partner.

Off your tucker: to have no appetite.

Old chook: a silly old woman.

Old crackers: elderly people.

Old fella: penis.

Olds: parents.

On a good wicket: doing well without too much effort.

On a sticky wicket: in trouble.

On the blink: not working reliably; about to break down.

On the bugle/nose: foul smelling.

On the make: seeking sexual conquest.

On the Murray cod: rhyming slang for on the nod; on credit.

On the outer: a pariah; to be rejected socially.

On the tin roof: something provided free of charge by the management.

On the turps: drinking heavily.

On the wagon: abstaining from alcohol.

On the wallaby track: travelling in the outback.

On the wrong tram: to be following a wrong train of thought; to misunderstand an issue.

On your Pat Malone: rhyming slang for on your own.

Once over (give it the): to check something thoroughly.

One-armed bandit: poker machine.

One up against your duckhouse: a setback.

Onkaparinga: brand of woollen blanket; rhyming slang for finger.

Onya!: good on you.

Ooroo!: goodbye.

Open slather: open to all comers; no restraints.

Optic nerve: rhyming slang for perve.

Op shop: opportunity shop, where second hand goods are sold.

Order of the boot: to be given the (Royal) order of the boot is to be fired from your job.

Organise a fart in a bean factory (couldn't): refers to someone who has no organisational skills whatsoever.

Organise a piss in a brewery (couldn't): refers to the same useless individual as above.

Organise a shit fight in a septic tank: the same disorganised person as above!

O.S.: overseas.

Out for lunch: lacking in intelligence or concentration.

Out of the box: exceptionally good; very special.

Out to grass: retired.

Out to it/out of it: totally drunk.

Outback: the desert heart of the continent, hot, remote and unhospitable country.

Outlaws: in-laws.

Oxford/Rhodes scholar: rhyming slang for dollar.

Oz: shorthand for Australia.

P

Pack of galahs: group of idiots.

Pack/cack your dacks: to be terrified.

Panic merchant: an individual who panics easily and tries to spread that panic.

Paper yabber: letter.

Paralytic: very drunk and unable to stand.

Park a tiger on the rug: to vomit.

Parrot mouth: a talkative person.

Paron's nose: the fatty nose-shaped end of a roast chicken.

Pash: a passionate kiss.

Pash on: behave in a passionate, sexual way with someone.

Pass over the Great Divide: to expire; to end.

Pat Malone: you are on your own/ alone.

Pav: short for pavlova, a meringue dessert.

Paw-paw: Queensland papaya (tropical fruit).

Pay through the nose: to part with too much cash; to pay more than something is worth.

Pearl: excellent.

Penguin: a nun.

Perk: a freebie; something for nothing that comes with your job; to vomit.

Perve: short for pervert; to ogle. *Come and have a perve at these norks, Bazza.*

Pester: annoy or bother someone.

Pick/pull the skin off a rice-pudding: refers to a weak or ineffectual person.

Piece of cake: an easy task.

Pie-eater: South Australian.

Piffle: nonsense.

Pig's bum: that's wrong; incorrect.

Pike out: to reneg on a deal or arrangement.

Piker: an individual who gives up or quits too easily.

Pinch: arrest.

Pint: large glass of beer, especially in South Australia.

Pipped at the post: narrowly beaten.

Piss: urine; to urinate; alcohol.

Pissed as a newt/parrot: drunk.

Pissed off: very annoyed.

Piss in someone's pocket: to crawl, or ingratiate yourself with someone.

Piss in the wind: to behave ineffectually.

Piss on you if you were on fire (wouldn't): refers to a mean person.

Pisspot: a heavy drinker.

Piss up: a party.

Plate of meat: your feet.

Play funny buggers: attempt to deceive.

Play possum: to pretend to be asleep.

Play the neddies: to gamble on horses.

Plonk: cheap wine.

Plum pud: rhyming slang for good.

Poddy dodger: cattle rustler.

Point Percy at the porcelain: to urinate in the toilet bowl.

Point the bone at: to predict failure; to blame someone.

Poison shop: a licensed hotel or bottle shop.

Poke in the eye with a sharp stick (better than): the situation is not ideal, but you will make the most of it.

Pokies: poker machines.

Pommie/Pom: an English person. Refers to Prisoner of Her Majesty, or Prisoner of mother England.

Pong: stink.

Poofter/poof: homosexual male.

Poohie: in a bad mood.

Pooned up: well dressed.

Possum: a loving nick or pet name.

Possum guts: a coward.

Postie: postman.

Possie: position; seating place.

Posh: well bred and very wealthy.

Pot: 285ml beer glass in Queensland and Victoria.

Pot calling the kettle black: someone said something adverse about you and you reply with this phrase (which says that they are the same or worse).

Pot hole: hole in the road.

Poxie/poxy: small, rubbishy and of poor quality.

Pozzie: position.

Prang: a minor car accident.

Prawn: shrimp.

Preggers: pregnant.

Pressies: gifts, presents.

Proddy-dog/prodhopper: old derogatory term used by Catholics or Protestants.

Proud as a rat with a gold tooth: someone who is very proud of how they look or something they have done.

Puffed: out of breath.

Pull a swifty: to trick someone.

Pull someone's leg: to play a trick on someone.

Pull the other one: I don't believe you!

Pull up your socks: get your life in order; get your act together.

Pull your head in mate: tell someone to mind their own business.

Pure merino: first class; excellent quality.

Purler: something that is great or excellent.

Purple patch: a run of good luck.

Push-bike: bicycle.

Push shit uphill with a sharp stick: to engage in a hopeless, impossible task.

Put a cork/sock in it!: shut up!

Put the bite on: to ask for a loan of money. *Davo put the bite on me for fifty bucks.*

Put the boot in: to attack someone when they are down.

Put the hard word on: to pressure someone.

Put the mockers on: to jinx or frustrate someone.

Put up job: a deceptive or contrived situation.

Put up your dooks!: to challenge someone to a fight.

Q

Qantas: originally Queensland and Northern Territory Air Service. The well-known Australian Airline with the flying red kangaroo as its emblem.

Quack: a doctor. *I felt crook so I went to the quack.*

Quaky Isles: New Zealand.

Quandong: a person who lives off others.

Quick snort: a rushed drink of alcohol.

Quid: former slang term for Australian pound which was superceded in the sixties by the dollar.

R

Rabbit: to tackle another player around the ankles (in football).

Rabbit killer: to hit someone on the back of the neck with the side of your hand.

Rabbit on: to natter mindlessly.

Racecourse emu: a punter who searches the racecourse grounds for discarded winning tickets.

Racing off: to have sex with someone else's wife or husband.

Rack off: get lost! *Rack off, Johnno!*

Rafferty's rules: a free for all; no holds barred.

Rag (the): newspaper; a woman who sleeps around.

Rage: party.

Raincoat: sometimes means a condom, depending on the context.

Raining cats and dogs: heavy rain/ storm.

Randy as mallee bull: sexually aroused.

Rank: stinks.

Rapt: to be very pleased with. *She was rapt with her present.*

Rare as rocking horse shit: very rare.

Ratbag: a scallywag, brat.

Rat shit/R.S.: no good.

Rattle your dags!: get a move on.

Ratty: snarky and unpredictable.

Reckon: to guess or estimate.

Reg Grundies: undies. Refers to a well-known former TV producer.

Rego: car registration.

Rellies: relatives.

Rhodes scholar: a top student; rhyming slang for dollar.

Richard Cranium: fancy way of saying Dick Head, which means idiot.

Ridgie-didge: the real thing; authentic.

Ring: centre of operations at a two-up school; backside.

Ringer: the fastest shearer in the shearing shed.

Ring-in: substitute, usually a last-minute arrangement.

Ripe (smells): smells off or bad.

Rip off: cheated.

Ripper: fantastic.

Ripper (you little): exclamation of delight.

Ripsnorter: excellent.

Road train: long haul, multi-wheel base vehicle usually encountered on remote highways.

Roam around like a lost sheep: to wander aimlessly or to be lost.

Roaring trade (doing a): doing a lot of business.

Roar the tripe out of: to give a dressing-down; to verbally abuse.

Rock, the: Uluru or Ayers Rock, the monolith in the Northern Territory.

Rock up: to turn up; to arrive. *Let's rock up to the pub at 11.*

Rollie: a hand-rolled cigarette.

Rolls canardly: a bomby car (it rolls down hills and can hardly get up them).

Roo: kangaroo.

Roo bar: large metal frame on the front of a vehicle for deflecting kangaroos in the bush. Also known as a bull bar.

Root: sexual intercourse.

Rooted: tired.

Ropable: very angry.

Rort: a rip off; a dodgy scheme.

Rotgut: awful cheap wine that feels like it's eating your stomach.

Rough as bags/rough as a pig's breakfast: uncouth; rude; lacking in finesse.

Rough end of the pineapple/stick: the poor end of a deal.

Rough nut: unsophisticated person.

Rough up: a noisy brawl.

Rouseabout: an odd job man.

Rubbity dub: rhyming slang for pub.

Ruby dazzler: an excellent person or thing.

Rugger bugger: a macho footballer.

Rug rats: children; babies.

Rug up: to dress warmly for cold weather.

Run about like a chook with its head cut off: to race around pointlessly.

Run around in the shower to get wet (have to): refers to a very thin person.

Run dead: to deliberately lose a race.

Run-in: argument.

Run like a hairy goat: to perform badly in a race.

Run like stink: to run fast.

Run of outs: to have a losing streak.

Run the rabbit: to obtain alcohol after hours.

Rush your fences: to act without thinking.

Rustbucket: a bomb of a car.

Rybuck: good; excellent.

Rybuck shearer: an expert shearer.

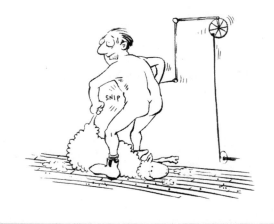

S

Sacked: fired from work.

Salvo: member of the Salvation Army.

Same diff: no difference, virtually the same thing.

Same here!: an expression of agreement.

Sammie: a sandwich.

Sandgroper: Western Australian.

Sandshoes: joggers, sneakers, trainers.

Sandwich short of a picnic: not quite all there mentally.

Sandy blight: an eye problem common in the outback caused by dust getting in the eyes.

Sandy McNab: rhyming slang for cab.

Sanga/er: sandwich.

Satdee: Saturday.

Sausage short of a barbecue: a dumb individual.

Scarce as hen's teeth: something extremely rare.

School at Christmas (like): has no class.

Schooner: a large beer glass in NSW and Qld, but a small beer glass in South Australia!

Scorcher: a very hot day; a very sexy date.

Scratchy: instant lottery ticket.

Scrub: bushland.

Scrubbers: wild cattle; promiscuous women.

Scrub-up well: to look good in formal or semi-formal wear.

Scumbag: a person of low morals.

Scunge: an individual who is derelict, unwashed and smells bad. Or to borrow (and normally not repay) a small amount of money or goods from someone.

Scungy: mean; a miserable portion.

See ya later: goodbye.

Seen his/her last gumtree: on the verge of death.

Sell ice to the Eskimos: the ability to sell anything to anyone, in particular things they do not need.

Selling tickets on himself/herself: a conceited, arrogant person.

Semi: semi trailer.

Septic tank: rhyming slang for Yank.

Servo: service station.

Settler's clock: kookaburra.

Shack: a crude kind of house or country cottage.

Shag: sexual intercourse.

Shaggin' wagon: panel van used for sexual exploits.

Shaky Isles: New Zealand.

Shank's pony: to travel on foot.

Sharkbait: someone who swims out beyond all the other swimmers at the beach.

Shark biscuit: somebody new to surfing.

Shearer's joy: beer.

Sheila: girl or woman.

She'll be right, mate: an assurance that things will work out.

Shepherd's friend: dingo.

Sherbert: beer.

Shickered: totally drunk.

Shifter/shifter brains: a stupid person.

Shindig: noisy party.

Shiny arse: public servant or politician.

Shiralee: swag (a rolled up blanket).

Shirty: short tempered; easily crossed.

Shit hot: very impressive.

Shit house: poor quality, unenjoyable. *The footy was shit house.* Also refers to a toilet.

Shit shoveller: menial labourer.

Shivoo: a wild party.

Shonky: dodgy, doubtful, unreliable.

Shook on: aroused by.

Shoot through: to leave suddenly to avoid paying a debt.

Short arms and deep pockets: an individual who will not part with their money, or won't buy a round when it's their turn.

Short and curlies: refers to pubic hair. To be held by the short and curlies is to be in a dire predicament.

Short arse: a short person.

Short of numbers in the Upper House: stupid.

Shot full of holes: very drunk.

Shot through like a Bondi tram: departed hastily.

Shout: to pay for a round of drinks.

Shouse: short for shit house, or toilet.

Shovel shit: to work in a menial job.

Sickie: day off work.

Silly as a two bob watch: to act crazy.

Silly sausage: a term usually applied to small children when they are being silly.

Silvertail: privileged member of the wealthy class.

Sin bin: a panel van fitted out for entertaining females and enjoying their favours.

Since Cocky was an egg: a long time ago.

Singlet: a tanktop; sleeveless undershirt.

Sink a few: to have a few drinks.

Sinker: a meat pie.

Sink the boot in: to kick someone violently; to attack verbally.

Sink the sav/sink the sausage: sexual

intercourse.

Sink the slipper: to kick during a fight.

Siphon the python: to urinate.

Sitting on an ant's nest: in a situation that is about to get worse.

Skedaddle: to leave in a hurry.

Skerrick: a very tiny portion; a smidgeon.

Skew-whiff: all awry; out of order.

Skinful: drunk.

Skinny as a sapling with the bark scraped off: very thin.

Skint: penniless.

Skite: braggart or show off.

Skittle: to knock something down.

Skull: to drink a whole bottle or glass of alcohol in one go, without taking a breath.

Sky pilot: clergyman.

Slab: a pack of 24 cans of beer.

Slacker: a lazy person.

Slag: a loose woman.

Slag off at: to pour contempt on.

Sleepout: closed in-house verandah, for extra bedroom.

Slow as a wet week in a caravan: painfully slow.

Sly grog: illegal alcohol.

Smack a blue: to strike trouble; get into a fight.

Smackers/smackeroos: money/dollars.

Smashed: drunk.

Smoko: a short break from work in which to smoke a cigarette.

Snag: sausage.

Snagger: a 'learner' shearer.

Snag short of a barbie: lacking in intelligence.

Snake juice: strong alcohol.

Snake's hiss: rhyming slang for piss.

Snaky: in a vile mood.

Snarler: sausage.

Snog: a passionate kiss.

Snow/snowy: nickname for a blonde or white haired person.

Snowdrop: to steal clothes from a washing line.

So low he could parachute out of the belly of a snake: refers to a person of low moral character.

So low he gets upgraded to economy class: refers to a person of low moral character.

So poor he/she woudl lick paint off the fence: very poor.

So slow he/she couldn't get a job as a speed hump: lethargic; slow witted.

So wet you could shoot ducks off him/her: idiotic.

Sook/sookybub: a wimp, someone who bursts into tears easily.

Soup strainer: a moustache.

Southerly Buster: a cool wind that blows up in Sydney after a hot spell.

Spag bol: spaghetti bolognese.

Sparkie: electrician.

Sparrow's fart: daybreak; first light of morning.

Speak into the big white telephone: to vomit into the lavatory.

Speedos: swim wear, generally men's bathers.

Speed merchant: a fast car driver.

Speewa: mythical outback location.

Spew: to vomit.

Spewin': very angry. *Stevo was spewin'!*

Spewy: unattractive; awful.

Spinebash: to sleep.

Spit chips: to express frustration.

Spit the dummy: to throw a tantrum. Refers to a baby refusing its pacifier, preferring to scream.

Splash the boots: to urinate.

Sponger: someone who lives off the efforts of others.

Spruiker: a person who touts with a loud hailer for business.

Sprung: caught in the act.

Spud: a potato.

Spunk: a sexy or desirable person of either sex.

Squatter: a person living on premises without permission.

Squatter's daughter: rhyming slang for water.

Square up: to set things right, make amends.

Squiz: a hurried look. *Take a squiz at this!*

Stack: to crash a car.

Stack your drapery: to put your coat on the ground before a fight.

Stands out like a black crow in a bucket of milk: obvious.

Stands/sticks out like a country dunny: immediately obvious.

Starkers: naked.

State election: rhyming slang for erection.

Station: large country property, usually with cattle or sheep grazing.

Steak and Kidney: rhyming slang for Sydney.

Sticks out like a dog's balls: blatantly obvious.

Stick your bib in: to interfere when not asked to.

Sticky tape: adhesive tape, also called Durex.

Sticky beak: a person who is overly curious or (verb) to inspect something closely. *I'll just go take a sticky beak at that new house.*

Stiff bickies: too bad.

Stiff cheddar: too bad, I have no sympathy!

Still kicking: alive.

Stingy: mean; ungenerous.

Stinker: a very hot day.

Stinko: smells; drunk.

Stirrer: an individual who deliberately or sometimes playfully causes trouble.

Stir the possum: to raise controversial issues; to create a disturbance.

Stockman: a station worker.

Stoked: extremely happy.

Stonkered: exhausted; drunk.

Stone the crows!: an expression of astonishment or frustration.

Stony/stony broke: penniless; broke.

Storm stick: umbrella.

Stoush: to punch or bash up.

Strain the potatoes: to urinate.

Strapped for cash: short of money; broke.

Stretch: nickname for a tall person.

Strewth!: another expression of surprise. Refers to *God's Truth!*

Strike a light: another expression of astonishment.

Strine: the Australian version of English.

Stroppy lorrakeet parade: general city traffic madness.

Stubbies: short shorts for blokes.

Stubby: a squat bottle of beer.

Stubby holder: polystyrene insulated holder for a stubby bottle or can.

Stuck-up: conceited.

Stuffed: very tired; useless and beyond repair.

Stunned: amazed; drunk.

Suck: an obnoxious person.

Sunbake: sunbathe; lie in the sun.

Sunbeam: a piece of crockery or cutlery that has not been used during a meal.

Sunday dog: a lazy person.

Sundowner: a lazy person; an organised get together after work.

Sunnies: sunglasses.

Super: superannuation or retirement pension.

Surfies: surfers.

Suss (a bit): probably of dubious origins; worthy of suspicion.

Suss out: to check something out to make sure it is all above board.

Swag: rolled up bedding as carried by a swagman.

Swaggie/Swagman: tramp; hobo.

Sweat on it: to wait apprehensively.

Sweet Fanny Adams: zilch; none; nothing.

Sword swallower: a person that eats off a knife.

Sydney Harbour: rhyming slang for barber.

Sydneyite: a resident of Sydney.

T

Ta: thanks.

T.A.B: Totalisator Agency Board, government controlled betting shops.

Take the piss out of: to be sarcastic towards.

Take a piece out of: to berate someone; give a piece of your mind.

Take a punt: to take a chance; to make a bet.

Take a shine to: to warm to something; to find a person likeable.

Take the mickey out of: to tease or ridicule someone.

Tall poppies: successful people.

Tall poppy syndrome: to criticise successful people.

Tally: to keep score.

Talk the lid off an iron pot: someone who talks a lot.

Talk under wet cement (can): refers to a person who never stops chattering.

Tanked: drunk.

Tart up: to do a superficial makeover.

Take a piece out of: to berate.

Tassie Tiger: someone from Tasmania.

Taswegian: a Tasmanian.

Tatty: ragged; shabby.

Technicolour yawn: vomit.

Tee up: to arrange something.

Telly: television.

Ten ounce sandwich: lunch consisting of only beer.

That's the way the Violet Crumbles: an observation on the way things have turned out. Refers to a honeycomb chocolate bar that shatters easily.

Thick as a brick: dull; slow witted.

Thick as two planks: not very bright; unintelligent.

Thingamajig: term used when you can't remember the real name.

Things are crook in Tallarook: times are pretty bad.

Thinks the sun shines out of his/her arse: to have high regard, usually exaggerated, for someone.

Thongs: rubber sandals (flip flops) with straps only between the first and second toes, usually worn to the beach.

Three parts gone: inebriated.

Throw your voice: to vomit.

Thunder box: outdoor toilet.

Thursdee: Thursday.

Tick: short period of time. *I'll be there in a tick (of the clock).*

Ticker: the heart.

Tickets on oneself (to have): to think you're great.

Tickle the till: to rob someone or a business.

Tide's gone out (the): your glass needs a refill.

Tighter than a fish's bumhole: a scrooge or miser.

Tin ear: an eavesdropper.

Tin lid: child; rhyming slang for kid.

Tinny: a can of beer; referring to someone who is uncannily lucky.

Tip the finger: to drink alcohol.

To go to town: to go hammer and tongs; to berate someone.

To have the trots: to suffer from diarrhoea; to have tickets on yourself: to be vain and conceited.

Toey: short tempered; impatient.

Togs: swimming costume.

Top End: Northern Territory.

Top Ender: Northern Territorian.

Too right!: definitely.

Tough as fencing wire: very rough.

Trackie daks/trackies: tracksuit pants.

Train choko vine over a country dunny (can't): refers to an ineffectual or weak person.

Trap for young players: a problem for novices or the unaware.

Trifecta: events that happen in threes, similar to a hat trick.

Trimmer: an excellent person or thing.

Triple fronted brick vanilla/venereal: cream brick dream home of the sixties.

Trooper: policeman.

Troppo: gone mad.

Trots: diarrhoea.

Trouble and strife: rhyming slang for wife.

Truckie: truck driver.

True blue: genuine.

Trunks: swimming shorts.

Tubes: large cans of beer.

Tucker: food.

Tucker bag: food bag.

Tucker chute: mouth.

Tuckshop: school canteen or cafeteria.

Tuesdee: Tuesday.

Tumble to: to become aware of.

Turn dingo: inform on others.

Turn it up!: exclamation of disbelief.

Turn-up for the books (a): a surprising outcome, from racing parlance.

Turps: a strong drink.

Twig: to suddenly comprehend.

Twit: an idiot.

Two pot screamer: a person who gets drunk easily.

Two men and a dog: poor attendance; very few people.

Two-up: an Australian gambling game where two coins are tossed with players betting on heads or tails.

U

Uluru: the Aboriginal and now common name for Ayres Rock.

Umpie: umpire.

Umpteen: a high number. *I've called him umpteen times and he's never home.*

Underdaks: underpants.

Underground mutton: rabbits.

Under the affluence of incahol: drunk.

Under the weather: ill or suffering a hangover.

Undies: underwear.

Unit: a small apartment or flat.

Up shit creek: everything going wrong.

Up the donga/donger: out in the country.

Up the duff: pregnant.

Up the gumtree: someone that got them self in a spot of trouble.

Up the pole: confused; incorrect.

Up the spout: ruined or pregnant.

Up yourself: to be conceited.

Up yours!: abusive term.

Up there Cazaly!: call of encouragement, referring to a legendary Australian Rules Footballer.

Useful as an ashtray on a motorbike: no use at all.

Useful as a flywire door on a submarine: useless.

Useful as a one legged man in an arse kicking contest: absolutely useless.

Useless as a handbrake on a Holden: serves no purpose; useless.

Useless as tits on a bull: no use at all.

Ute: utility vehicle, Australian equivalent of a pick-up truck.

Uwie (uee, uie): a u-turn.

Vandyke: outdoor lavatory

Veggies: vegetables.

Veggo: vegetarian.

Vee dub: a Volkswagen car.

Vegemite: an Australian vegetable yeast extract spread for bread and biscuits.

Veg out: to rest and relax.

Verandah above the toyshop: a large belly on a man.

Verbal diarrhoea: never-ending blather.

Village bike: a promiscuous woman.

Vino: cheap wine.

Visiting card: an article of clothing or object recognisable as belonging to a certain person.

Volcanoes: pimples or boils.

Vulture: a driver that double parks; someone that hangs over another's shoulder while waiting for something.

W

WACA: (pronounced whacker) acronym for the Western Australian Cricket Association and the Perth cricket ground.

Wacker: a crazy person.

Waffle: to talk nonsense.

Wag: to play truant from school.

Wake up Australia!: said to someone daydreaming or not concentrating.

Walkabout: the practice of going bush for an unscheduled time away.

Walkabout (gone): lost.

Walking ticket: to get laid off from your job.

Walkover: something that is done easily or someone deceived easily.

Wallaby track: to go on this track is to go wandering in search of a job.

Walloper: a policeman.

Wally: an idiot; someone that forgot something.

Wally Grout: rhyming slang for shout.

Waltzing Matilda: to carry a swag, also a famous Australian song.

Wank: to masturbate.

Wanker: someone who is obviously in love with themself.

Waterhole: the local pub.

Water the horse: to urinate.

Weak as a wet whistle: very weak.

Weak as piss: without strength; having no substance.

Weatherboard: wooden house.

Wedding tackle: penis.

Weed: tobacco but now more commonly used for marijuana.

Wee wee: pee pee.

Were you born in a tent?: said to someone who continually leaves the door open.

Wellies: Wellington boots; gum boots; waterproof boots.

Well under: drunk.

Welsh on: inform on someone; to fail to pay debts; to betray.

Went through like a dose of salts: to leave quickly.

Westie: someone from the Western suburbs.

Wet (the): monsoon season in the tropical north.

Wet as water: ineffective.

Wet enough to bog a duck: extremely wet weather.

Whacko!: excellent!

Wharfie: waterside worker.

What do you do for a crust?: what do you do for a job?

What's the damage: how much do i owe you?

What's your beef?: what's your problem?

Wheelie: the noisy practice of spinning the wheels of a car by accelerating suddenly.

When the eagle shits: pay day.

When the shit hits the fan: when a problem occurs.

Whinger: a whiner; complainer.

Whinging pom: a complaining English immigrant.

Whippersnapper: a child; a cheeky young person.

Whirl (give it a): give it a go.

White-ant: to attempt to ruin another's chances. *He white-anted the proposal.*

White pointer: highway patrol.

White pointers: lady sunbaking topless.

Whiz (to take a): urinate.

Whizzer: penis.

Whoopydoo!: an exclamation of delight, but sometimes sarcastic.

Whopper: something enormous.

Who's robbing this coach?: said when someone is interfering.

Why keep a dog and bark yourself?: said to someone that does a task that someone else should do.

Widgie: a female 'bodgie'.

Wig-wam/wing-wong for a goose's bridle: frustrated parents' explanation to a persistently questioning child. *And what's that, Daddy? It's a wig-wam for a goose's bridle, son.*

Willies: anxieties, apprehension. *That bloke gives me the willies.*

Willy: penis.

Willy-willy: small dusty whirlwind.

Windy enough to blow a blue dog off its chain: extremely windy.

Within cooee: near, close. Refers to a traditional bush call for help when lost (coo-ee!). *I came within a cooee of winning that prize.*

Wobbly (to chuck a): to throw a tantrum. Similar to *chuck a spaz.*

Wog: a stomach virus; fly larvae; souther European native.

Wombat: refers to a male Casanova. A wombat is a native Australian animal.

Wonky: unsteady on the feet.

Won't have a bar of: refuses to have anything to do with, rejects.

Wooden spoon: the award for coming last in the sports table.

Wool chaser: a dog that bites sheep.

Woolloomooloo uppercut: a kick to the groin.

Woolly woofter: rhymes with poofter, which is a term for a male homosexual.

Woop-woop: any remote location.

Woop-woop pigeon: a kookaburra.

Would bet on two flies crawling up a wall: refers to a compulsive gambler.

Would knock your socks off: something amazing.

Would talk a glass eye to sleep: a boring person.

Wouldn't give you the time of day: an uncooperative person.

Wouldn't it rot your socks off!: something very annoying or disgusting.

Wouldn't know him if I found him in my Cornflakes packet: a complete stranger.

Wouldn't know his arse from his elbow: a stupid individual.

Wouldn't know if he was Arthur or Martha: an idiot; someone so drunk they don't know where they are.

Wouldn't shout in a shark attack: a selfish person.

Wouldn't touch with a ten-foot pole: will have nothing to do with it.

Wouldn't use him/her for sharkbait: to hold someone in very low regard.

Wouldn't work in an iron lung: a very lazy individual.

Wowser: killjoy, spoilsport, anti-drinking, anti-fun individual.

Write-off: a car damaged in an accident beyond repair. Refers to the insurance company writing the vehicle off as a loss.

XXXX: (pronounced Four X) brand of beer made in Queensland.

Y

Yabber: to natter, to talk.

Yabbie: small fresh water crayfish.

Yacking: talking a lot.

Yahoo: wild larrikin.

Yakka: hard work. Refers to a brand of tough work wear.

Yanking my chain: telling a lie.

Yank tank: a large American car.

Yarn: a story or to have a good talk with someone.

Yellow fever: gold fever; gold prospecting.

Yobbo: uncouth individual; a lair.

Yodel: to vomit.

Yonks: a long time. *I haven't seen him in yonks.*

Yonnie: a small, smooth, flat stone perfect for skimming across the surface of water.

You beaut!/You little beauty!: a jubilant exclamation.

You'd make a blowfly sick: used as an insult.

Your blood's worth bottling: said to someone that has done something excellent or that you admire.

Youse: plural of you.

Yowie: mythical creature. Like big foot or a yeti.

Z

Zs (catch some): sleep.

Zack: sixpence (pre-decimal equivalent to 5 cents).

Zebra crossing: striped lines across a road, indicating where pedestrians can cross.

Ziff: a beard.

Zilch: zero, nothing.

Zonk: a fool.

Zonked: exhausted, totally worn out.

AUSSIE SLANG DICTIONARY

Lolla Stewart

ISBN 9781925367669   Qty

                                    RRP   AU$17.99   .....

Postage within Australia   AU$5.00   .....

                                    TOTAL★ $_____

                                    ★ All prices include GST

Name:...

Address: ....

....

Phone:...

Email: ....

Payment: ❑ Money Order ❑ Cheque ❑ MasterCard ❑Visa

Cardholders Name:...

Credit Card Number: ....

Signature:..

Expiry Date: ....

Allow 7 days for delivery.

Payment to: Marzocco Consultancy (ABN 14 067 257 390)
                   PO Box 452
                   Torquay Victoria 3228
                   Australia

Be Published

Publish through a successful publisher.
Brolga Publishing is represented through:
• National book trade distribution, including sales,
marketing & distribution through Simon & Schuster.
• International book trade distribution to:
     - The United Kingdom
     - North America
     - Sales representation in South East Asia
• Worldwide e-Book distribution

For details and enquiries, contact:
Brolga Publishing Pty Ltd
ABN 46 063 962 443
PO Box 452
Torquay Victoria 3228
Australia

markzocchi@brolgapublishing.com.au
(Email for a catalogue request)